Sam I Am

Poems of God's Love

by Scott A. Miller

For Passion Publishing Company

Bellingham, Washington U.S.A.

Copyright © 2018, Scott Alan Miller

All rights reserved. No part of this book may be reproduced or transmitted in any form or by any means, electronic or mechanical, including photocopying, recording, or by any information storage and retrieval system, without permission in writing from the publisher.

First Edition.

ISBN 978-0-692-19877-3

LCCN: 2018911913

Printed in the United States of America.

Dedication

I dedicate this book to my girls...

Crystal

Ann

Katie

May

Jodi

Lee

Acknowledgments

I wish to personally thank the following individuals who without their loving support this book of poetry would not have been written:

My special thanks goes to Mom and Dad, James and Beverly Miller. My mom was a painter and taught tole painting and had a little shop in Redondo, Washington called The Salt Box, and the art work on the cover is one of her paintings, as well as the back cover. She was also a school teacher of 5th and 6th grade.

I also want to thank my Auntie Sharley and Unkle Bill for all they have done for my mom and dad for so many years. I love them dearly.

A special thanks goes to my cousin, Vicki Waggoner, who has also been there for my mom and dad, and me as well

I also want to thank, in memory of, Diane Ruiz who always encouraged me to write a book of poetry.

Also, my new precious grandbabies have inspired me to get started and finish my book...Serena, Isaac, and Amy.

My gratitude extends to Dr. Daniel Levine of For Passion Publishing for editing, coordinating all the aspects of the book, and publishing. It was a pleasure working with Daniel, who exemplifies the idea that professionalism and kindness are compatible behaviors.

I also appreciate the dedication of my layout and design technician, Zander Levine, for expert technical book publishing skills.

Of course, I am also grateful to the good people at Village Books in Fairhaven, Bellingham, who set me on the right path to realizing my dream that I could be a published poet. Thank you, Jes Stone and Candee Blanc.

About the Author

I was born in Seattle, and raised in Redondo Beach. It was a thrill to be close to Puget Sound. I was baptized at 14 years old, and when I fell in love, the poems started to flow.

I have had a good life, even now just blessed at all the good things that have happened to me.

My poetry is about my life's journey and my walk with God. I was blessed with happy, healthy girls, who have turned out to be amazing women, and I am very proud of them and dedicate this book of God's love to them.

I hope you will find a poem that you like, or maybe even saves a soul along the way.

God bless, Scott.

Table of Contents

Morning Love	1
Deeper	2
Friendship to Me	3
Heaven	4
Deeper	5
Reaching Eyes	6
My Angel	7
Solid Soul	8
Staircase	9
Over There	10
Pattern of Life	11
Just Three	12
Bridge the Gap	13
That Dream	14
Part	15
Starlings	16
Shameless Heart	17
Drifting	18
Rain	19
Drunken Driver	20
Twist of Life	21
Cold Days	22
Dream	23
My Soul	24
A Life in a Day	25
Tiny Hearts	26
Hidden Thoughts	27
Seven Years	28
Yes, Dear	29
The Gloomers	30

Real Life	31
I Love You, Dad	32
One More Day	34
Helpless Martian Man	35
My Friend	36
Black Beauty	37
Choice	38
Just Ten	39
The Thrill	40
Sunny Day	41
New Life	42
Soul Contusion	43
Just Be	44
One Path	45
3 Starlings	46
Clear Eyes	47
Desires	48
Just Soul	49
My Angel	50
My Father	51
Gift	52
Time	53
Change	54
Revelation	55
My Dad	56
Humble	57
I'm Not Far From Home	58
Just Go	59
Spilt Milk	60
Far Away	61
Just Your Life	62
Hear to See	63

Melissa	64
Precious Souls	65
Your Light	66
True Face	67
Lean	68
Share	69
Choose	70
Jodi	71
Angel Hands	72
My Friend	73
Just Pure	74
Peace of Love	75
Never Alone	76
Soul Be True	77
Humble Am I	78
Make Amends	79
Real	80
Gathering	81

Morning Love

Calm is the crystal clear water of the ocean,
the fragrance of the fresh air,
and at times, the bitter cold
within the dew-dripped mornings.

As the searching sun begins to rise,
filling the dark with light,
sharing its warmth with whoever can feel it inside.

At this time the birds begin to sing
their morning love as they do each day of their life,
expressing their beauty to all,
as beauty was theirs when they were born.

It tends to calm toward half-day before sun fall,
as a rest sets in before darkness.
This is just God's way of saying
there shall be another tomorrow.

Deeper

How deep can one feel with what love they know?
How much it can hurt when unable to grow.
Someday they say, your love will come,
only to fear of being unwanted.

Loneliness is the feeling of being alone,
alone with no one to care for as much as they care for you.
That deepness gets closer to me each day I live,
trying to anyone love I can give.
But expressing just to anyone is that
fear that can grow of not being loved.
Although I can always love,
only my heart grows weaker from being alone.

Friendship to Me

The warmth you feel when they're around,
the touch of love that's there to be found,
an open heart with open eyes,
the soft and pure feeling that closely ties.

Oh, for the trusting love I feel,
honest, respectful, yet close and real,
a laugh, a cry expresses to me why,
someone to turn to when not feeling so high.

Beauty and breeze put together as one,
true friends forever will always have fun.
When the time comes in life
for you to go your own way,
someday, someday I say
you see in my eyes
that is friendship to me.

Heaven

Thoughts of you run through my mind,
like that of rain through a rainbow,
enjoy what you see and don't let life go
by too slow.

As the sun breaks over the cloud,
my heart enters a calming.
It makes me want to wait,
to wait for what you bring.

Take a walk, hold a hand,
run your naked toes through the silty sand,
as you feel the warmth to your face,
you think, but is there a better place,
a better place to be,
a different life to see.

We enter each day to feel a certain way,
to work real hard or play,
we sometimes drift away.

To know there is a God somewhere
to know He will guide us there,
where rainbows are forever,
and you never feel cold.

So lift your eyes, and feel His Spirit in your heart,
live good and pray some day
He will let you take part,
take part in what will be grand
to enter a life, someday what we feel,
live on after man.

Deeper

Deeper I go, wanting to grow,
wanting to show my love.
Give me a chance or some hope within,
give it a chance for this love to begin.

What fun it could be just not loving one,
but oh what loneliness will always overcome.
You fear different people,
and what they can do,
you crawl up in a corner
afraid to be you.

Can't you see what I want,
won't you search me inside?
Please don't be afraid,
please don't run and hide.

Whatever love I show
accept this as friendship from me.
Someday they might understand,
someday they might be able to see.
At times I often wonder
who was meant for me in life,
Will our love be free
or will our love be a strife.

I guess you can say I'm afraid
and insecure of my future unknown.
But I've learned in the past how to love,
and I'm not afraid to show.

You see, all I want from life
is another to love me within.
I feel with this special hope,
life, I've already begun to win.

Reaching Eyes

Have you seen the pain of others on TV and all around?
Devastation, sometimes death, a shame that's all they found
Where do they go from here, how can they even start?
What pain they must feel, such a burden on their heart.

As people we come together, seems fair and the only way to be
If we shun away from problems, more hurt inside we see.
so just let go and help others get un-sad,
the future is all we have.

Our young will lead our countries,
the unhappy could soon be glad.
Like the wet of the rain as you walk,
yet the sun is there to warm.
It's like the black of darkness,
it's deepest before the dawn.

Share and care...
We should all do our part,
real people, real love,
must always begin in the heart.

My Angel

Out of all the ones I've loved,
out of all the ones I've seen,
you were the first one to bless me,
the first one God let me see.

My life has changed so much,
without you I was lost.
Never let me go,
'cause Crystal, you're my angel,
and without you, I would have never really grown.

Solid Soul

Do what you want with the love you feel,
bare your soul, share what's real.
When given the chance, give what you got,
it might not be much, but it sure is a lot!

The soul you bear, is the one you share,
has there ever been another way?
Don't be shy of God's love,
don't push Him away...
connect with His favor of love...
be a solid soul and let Him
show you the way!

Staircase

In your staircase of life, do you see the sun?
Is it the beach that gives you fun,
or the water that helps you be one?
Mankind has lived without this dream,
pushing progress over what I've seen.

A fog-spread morning with the sun rising tall,
just years later and bulldozers covering all.
Although a memory not soon to forget,
that bulldozer of life, wrecked that staircase I bet.

I've been there, I've seen
what rich people do, it sure can be mean.
They sacrifice all not to question the past,
that memory of the staircase
with me will always last.

Forget the rising costs,
a vision and they will never see.
The staircase is gone,
the wood will never be.

A view, a tub, and court
will replace this vision I hold.
Too bad they didn't care about the staircase
when the property was sold.

Over There

Haven't you heard, haven't you seen,
just another world going mean.
What does it take,
what can I do,
to make it a better place
for me and you?

I can hear, and you can wonder,
why can't life be like a hot steamy summer?
A place far away, we are always looking forward,
the stars, the moon, the sun,
is what I'm reaching toward.

In this life we're taught to share,
but haven't you heard and haven't you seen
no one will help that man over there...

Pattern of Life

This pattern of life,
getting stronger, staying real,
like a bird flying high,
what does it feel?

It can sense danger,
it can flee from harm,
flying high above
it can do no wrong.

Like this love we breed,
we act on hope,
to fulfill our need.
We share our thoughts,
and to share our dreams,
flying high above,
it's a pattern I see.

Just Three

Three of the night,
simple and sigh –
don't hang up,
'cause it's a night that never dies.
Don't be safe,
your eye only sees blue,
to me, to you,
to see, to do.

Washing down the waves
you only get wet on the scene.
Freaking out your mama,
growing a natural bean.
Psychedelic powers never seen before but felt,
whisper waters of change,
three of the night I hold,
three of the night I'm dealt.

Bridge the Gap

Bridge the gap to heaven,
you are the only one that can.
Look past your own desires,
with Jesus we have a plan.

Those eyes that you feel are on you,
they will never go away,
the path to the Lord's glory,
shall be the only way.

So bridge those gaps of life,
we know many will refuse to cross...
Just bridge the gap to Heaven,
before your soul is lost.

That Dream

Simple is the night,
when I wake you from your dream.
You bolted straight up next to me,
I'll never forget that scream.

You said it was water
just over your head,
can't reach the light,
I soon will be dead.

I thought of you and what we have seen,
missing you soon was not in my dream.
When God needs me
in His house of light,
and I've drifted to where it's real.

Please don't awake me from this dream I've had,
you need to die to get there I feel.

Part

We seem to go through the days,
and never know,
and some never seem to care,
some are never there,
some can't even bear,
what the last tune will be.

It will be of the past,
but then of the now.
Based on your thoughts and again of the how.

Be a part, make a new start.
Accept the changes, embrace your heart.
Know that life has days
that never seem to start,
when the last tunes are playing,
pray you are a part.

Starlings

It's hard I know,
with some people I've seen--
they're out there
for what they can get,
it seems to always turn mean.

So do you know
what I saw today?
I saved three starlings
in some kind of way.
So mean don't bother me
I'm too busy to see,
what's so high above
I know in me, my God believes.

Shameless Heart

As each day passes,
a new day of changes will come,
different faces, different places,
sometimes you just want to run.

Enjoy I say, what you see and feel,
don't be afraid,
and let life be so real.

And if a smile passes your way,
try and pass the same.
It shares your heart inside
and it shows you have no shame.

To ever be at loss with life,
just remember the struggle and the strife.
To work so hard and pray,
good things will come your way.

When the sun shines,
the warmth reaches my ever-so-hidden heart.
I wish I could release
and find a way to make a start.

The start to a better life,
where I never want to run,
when a smile is like the sun,
with true warmth in everyone.

This day could be hidden like my heart,
only hoping to reach that time,
to share with another soul,
one as special and real as mine.

  I'll always do my best
  and know I am in God's eyes.
  Going to heaven starts in your heart,
  and is something you could never buy.

Drifting

The smoke coils,
you drifted again.
You created a life,
don't run,
it's about to begin.

Lift your eyes
the Creator of all,
thank God every moment
when you stumble and fall.

Hurt creates desires,
that we pull deep within
a severed soul,
a simple sin.

Don't look now,
you drifted again,
my feet on this fresh cut grass,
how nice it feels,
just stepped on a bee,
reality becomes real.

Rain

When you walk through the park
in the rain and the dark,
do you feel on the edge of the moment?

You can reach but never fall
to the skies were one as all
but it's always just for the moment.

Like a dry place to hide,
just a good feeling inside,
let's walk a little more through the dark.

It's just a park,
just a park in the rain,
through the dark.

When the sun finally shines
to dry and take its place,
when the shadow in the deepest of darkest
is no longer there on your face.

Don't go back where you came
'cause it might not ever change,
in that park where it's dark
wet with rain.

Drunken Driver

When I was 10 it was easier then,
in touch with only how to play.
One day I was told this was all changing soon,
and my parents have gone away.

What did I say to make them leave,
what did I do to make them go?
The ones who are there are not anywhere,
that's all I really know.

Somehow it's different right now,
growing up eating grandma's soup.
No more playing, she said, get to work,
it's the only way to take away the hurt.

What did I say to make them leave,
what did I do to make them go?
The ones who were there, are not anywhere,
that's all I need to know.
On my own now,
and it's never made sense,
until I learned how much it was a shame.
All these years when I thought it was my fault,
but a drunk driver who feels the same
what did he do to make them leave,
what did he do to make them go?
Just another drunk driver on the streets,
that's all I'll ever know.

Twist of Life

Every corner,
most places you go,
life has a twist,
don't you know.

If bill ain't written,
the dog is there bitten.
Madness does it seem,
the twisting of life,
bustin' at the seam.

The roads we travel
should always be shining bright,
every corner, every place
just a twist of life.

Some will run,
but most can't hide,
because the twist of life
has a rising tide.

Twist, tear, and take,
it's up to you
to drive this road of fate

Cold Days

If the days were to grow cold,
what would you bring.
When the snow was blowing hard,
where would you sing?

I know, it's a place I see,
a God calling on you, and
calling on me.

Don't be afraid,
it's what to be.
My God calling on
you and calling on me.

The blow of cold
might be the state you're in,
the days could get warm
if you let go of the sin.

Please help me now,
as the cold sets in,
believe in you,
I always will win.

Dream

I see a dream,
I know is there,
can't wait to see
what I know is there...

It's a mountain,
a river,
I feel I've been there before,
such a place,
such a dream,
a true love we need to know.

In this dream,
I am happy and warm in my soul,
complete and done
and ready to go...

It's not just a dream,
it's a mountain,
a river,
and a cool running stream.

My Soul

Admission to my soul is ever so free,
show me parts of you,
I'll show a part of me.

Like a smile and a laugh
and the real we hold inside,
give me that hand of friendship,
it's an admission I can not hide.

People as people wonder why,
and why are they so cruel?
It is something you are taught to learn--
some blame it on the world.

Our eyes can say a lot,
and show it deep within.
Do you walk with angels in life,
or do you walk with sin?

My soul never wonders just once,
do I reach or will I know?
I never question my heart,
I would never question my soul.

A Life in a Day

What a thrill you'll never know
the places I've been, the places I go.
When it started one year and until this day
it has been what I've done, it has been my way.

The different faces, the crowds all around
to do something different is yet to be found.
When you find what you like and the things it has done,
it's hard to change a thing when you're having fun.

People see you risking your life
high in the sky so blue
for they would rather sit,
it is something they could never do.

So just a prayer as I start my day—
what thrills I might endure
Because climbing is my forte.

That is one thing that's for sure,
working and climbing trees is fun,
 it's like going out to play.
If you ever feel like I do,
you have just spent a life in a single day.

Tiny Hearts

As the time and distance grow farther away,
a tear will fall to start my day.
Words could never express or share,
of those little hearts I miss,
and for who are not there.

It seems as just a thought,
as I feel your smile,
and hear your laugh
our distance for ever not.

As each day slips by I know
you're both so very loved,
as I stand above so tall,
I know without me you would surely fall.

So together we shall stay strong
apart our lives will seem long,
as I pray for that day real soon,
when I can hold that tiny hand,
and your cries fill that small room.

If your heart starts to hurt and sigh,
just remember those sunny days
that seem to just go by
and the fun we shared those times.

Five days may not seem long
of the time we will miss together.
It's as if we were in space,
a forever drifting feather.

So just be strong my babies,
for Daddy will feel your love close to me.
Someday you will know how much I loved you,
Someday soon I hope you see.

Hidden Thoughts

Your smile shares your heart,
although just a simple part,
comes ever so free.

Your eyes are filled with desire and hope,
and shows one of your best parts to be.
It might be just a thought,
but when it's of you it's very pure,
and one of love.

As you swiftly move through your day
of troubles or relax,
always take the time to sigh
a breath of contentment.

As you spoke to me,
no truer words could be.
Take the time,
a person should need,
maybe share with another,
maybe quietly read.

For what life has to offer
we all do our part,
the ones who live on forever,
love always comes from their heart.

Honestly hope I've found a good friend in you,
just know I'm tired of being blue.
But I'll always have a smile,
and a happy thought to share,
it's just thoughts of you that are so easy,
through my Lord to bear.

Seven Years

How do you let go of seven years of life,
why do I justify each day since,
what's wrong and what is right?

The pain is so bad it hurts more with every day,
trying to go in different directions
hoping for a better way.

Love is like the weather,
sometimes good, sometimes bad,
but real love that comes from your heart,
is real feelings you always will forever have.

I guess I should just move on,
and give all my love to my kids,
for I know they will always be there,
I know they will always care.

So when the time comes in life
to share with another,
I would never run to hide in a storm
if the love was like the weather,
always care, always be there forever.

Yes, Dear

And it's been hard, when I get up with you,
all the jobs that you make me do.
You point your finger and say,
"I want it over there,
then there's the laundry
and the dishes, too,
don't forget the bed,
have you made it yet?"

I guess I'm having trouble
being a "Yes, Dear" kinda man…
You holler at me when the football's on
and say to me, "Is the vacuuming done?"
then you shake your head
as you walk away from me.

I guess I'm just not the "Yes, Dear" type,
"Get this done,"
then she says, "It's not right."
I point my finger and say,
"Football's over there."
It's been hard to be a "Yes, Dear" kinda man…

The Gloomers

Gloom and doom,
what-a-ya-do?
Gonna let it crawl on your back,
take hope away from you?

These ones that are around us
who have no faith inside,
can't let 'em invade my light,
their darkness always survives...

So please save that doom and despair
for a soul who you think's on a mission.
my Lord will feed me the Light,
it's the faith in my God I listen--

Real Life

As you smile,
I see your pain.
Inside, you're weak from the game,
you search, you try,
and you can't help not to cry.

As the days go by,
you ask yourself and wonder,
what would be different,
what chance will change if you do what's pondered,
if you search too deep you sometimes get caught,
caught like a fish, caught forever not.

Your pain can be healed if you search
and love your heart,
without a personal closeness,
it's hard to make a start.

I think life is what you make it,
through your eyes as you breathe,
it's sad to think we could exit this world
when it's not your time to leave.

I guess what I'm trying to say
is to deal with life in a special way,
to live and to love,
and to feel like you're special,
in a good kind of way.

People need people,
and should not be afraid to show.
Because the bottom line is
we must make our marks before we go.

I Love You, Dad

I remember the tickle monster,
who tickled me on the ground,
I remember thinking,
"I sure do have the best dad around".

I remember Skagit Speedway,
it was so loud, yet so fun,
loving every moment of it,
wondering when it will be done.

I remember roasting marshmallows,
over a summer night campfire,
enjoying it with my dad,
there is nothing more that I desired.

I remember my early teen years,
when all I thought about was me,
not considering what I do,
not willing to even see.

Throughout my life,
we come to know one thing,
I'll always love my dad,
no matter what this life might bring.

He's been there through the good times,
and even in the bad,
as cliché as this may sound,
he **IS the Number 1 Dad!**

As I grow and learn,
and the pages of my life continue,
Dad, you'll always have a role to play,
to always be a part in my life, I pray.

Thank you for the love you gave,
it has molded me to who I am today.
I know that through rough and bumpy parts,
after all, life will be okay.

God has a plan for you,
for His children does He love,
He watches over us,
and sends us angels from above.

I love you, Dad,
you help me more than you may know,
I love you, Dad,
way more than I may show.

One More Day

Well, can you say you made it just another day,
was everything moved from your way,
if it's not one thing it's another, I know.

When it's smooth like a nice running car,
you oughtta know you won't get too far.
But if you do you thank God anyway.

Just give me a reason to carry on,
gotta be more to life than just mowing the lawn.

I've seen the big fancies with their suits and ties,
Success with you is where the heart lies.
So take another day to make your way,
take the time and say it's just another day.

Helpless Martian Man

Can you believe it, I did it again,
I trusted a heart, I let a new start begin.

We ran through the rain of life,
we shared our thoughts and dreams,
we held each other close,
the end it never seemed.

But you changed it in a way I know,
exposed to a way never seen.
Your hateful words don't hurt,
you certainly haven't shattered my dreams.

Where I draw the line
is when you smashed something dear, you see.
When you crushed my guitar,
you broke part of me.

My Friend

Another day has gone by,
without seeing my friend.
I know I should stop by
to see how it's been.

I figure he's real busy,
but so am I.
Never thought I'd turn the corner,
and almost see him die.

You have no idea
what went through my head,
Is he alive?
Please, Lord, don't let him be dead.

It just goes to show,
with friends that really care,
the memory of them laughing,
all of a sudden they're not there.

Black Beauty

We once ran free, never knowing just the same.
Going from field to field, running through
the steadfast rain.

Sold as a piece of life,
Giving to your selfish needs.
Sometimes slaughtered or eaten,
keeping only the better breeds.

Just let me know, I'm as free as I feel,
To run real fast, to climb that hill.
Don't take me away to another farm or home,
Just keep me here where I'm free to roam.

When I get the chance to break and be free,
I'd chase that lass, the one I'd hoped to see.
She's by a field and a cool running stream,
Please somebody help me not awaken from this dream.

Choice

Have you made your choice,
have you lived real good,
is God's spirit alive in you,
have you done all that you could?

To help the ones around,
there's always such a need,
true hope in the Lord's love,
is all I really see.

The choice to give is there,
that's all He really wants,
be a soul that gives,
not the one who wants.

It's a simple choice we make,
just how you live your life,
sharing the glory of God,
making the choice that is right.

Just Ten

"Oh, you're ten,"
say again
but you're young enough,
to see it begin.

Know what's right,
do what's wrong,
grow up fast,
grow up strong.

Life is not a painted sunny day,
life is full if you make it that way.

You smile, and cry,
and ask life "Why?"
You laugh, and shrug
and just get by.

What's the thoughts of you when 10,
Oh, gee, that was fun,
Can I do that again?

Learn what you see,
and be part of me.
Learn what you know,
and see how to grow.

The Thrill

It's a thrill of a life to learn,
seems a chance to always take.
Hope's not always wondered,
to reach love not always made.

Have a touch to give,
give a chance to take,
our life's our family,
our friends real love is what should be made.

Out of this I feel could heal,
your pain or hurt inside,
just run with me someday
when I feel I might hurt or hide.

Through the heart were all the same,
with bitter love there's always blame.
Don't let hate fall to shame.
Can't you see what's to be?

Always smile, always care,
if you can through the often unfair.
It's just nice to know we could enter a world
much greater than our own,
someplace God calls His home.

I will always reach to others,
I will always try to care.
Just tired of being alone
with no one ever there.
Just makes me stronger inside,
and I would never run and hide,
from a real love someday
I will find.

Sunny Day

Remember the good old ways
of a sunny day,
never seem to end,
forever always play.

Runnin' to the ice cream man,
telling him to wait,
beggin' mom for a quarter,
but she says you haven't ate.

Oh, please let me stay late,
just once tonight.
Don't want to be home when you and Dad
go through your fight.

My little brother has to run home from school,
he says they all hate him, and he's not being cool.
A wish is all it takes to just make it go away,
so don't forget the good old ways, of a sunny day.

For the past has a piece of us,
showing us the way,
just the good old ways,
the good old ways of a sunny day.

New Life

When will I know,
when will it be right?
Life's not always a struggle,
life's not always a fight.

As the reaching light starts another day,
as life's fight begins to get in my way.
Just sit back with the smile I just shared,
just an honest soul I bared.

Don't be afraid to look back and see,
set it to the heart, set it ever so free.
Grab your heart with both your hands,
sheltered from the cold.
Make your way through darkness,
rely on the convictions you've been sold,

be set right,
tonight don't forget what's yours,
for tomorrow could always bring
a new set of opened doors.

Soul Contusion

Just a state of confusion,
not a broken heart,
but a soul contusion.

Gain strength from that nasty fall down the hill.
Make life worth living, and not a living hell.

When a bird dies,
a spirit is lifted to the sky.
If evil drips from your pores,
you surely will fry.

Not a broken heart,
but a soul contusion,
not a waste of time,
but a dose of life's illusion.

Just Be

Have you been a part of me,
have you been a part of you?
When the Lord has guided your heart,
to do the things you should.

Does it come so fast you can't wait,
to give what God has sent.
Running past any doubt,
knowing that it was meant!

To be a part of me,
is an honor that many will never see.
Faith, our love, and hope,
is God's vision for us...
Let it be.

One Path

Stay strong, and right with your soul,
in this challenge that has forced its way.
God's plan for this choice to come…
will lead you too, to see His way.

Stay on the good path,
and know "It is always there."
Hard choices can be our battle,
but when you give it to the Lord,
that is when it matters.

3 Starlings

Do you know what I saw today?
Three starlings flying away.
I almost saw a life change
in some kind of way.

How do you feel
when a smile comes to you?
Do you smile back,
do you give one, too?

I feel in life when you reach
to what's always right,
you avoid the daily struggles,
there is no fight.

So you know what I saw today,
three starlings flying away.

Clear Eyes

In my eyes I see a change,
can only be for good.
For most of life's lessons,
your clear and understood.

Just a breath of air,
to make us feel alive,
the pressure of a day
in our heart we need to strive.

Can only do once,
what most of us need twice,
some people sacrifice love,
and pay a dear price.

Be one of the few,
let your eyes see and do,
don't sacrifice your heart,
remember all you have been through.

Desires

If there was ever a moment of doubt
in your mind you could do without.
You take and sing your song,
I'll be there hummin' along.

Oh, for the simple loves I see,
help it along, and help it be.

Don't ever let me wonder
if it's just a game,
let the one who knows you the best,
just feel the same.

There's no moment of doubt,
in this game.
All there is, is my desire,
I hope you feel the same.

Just Soul

If there is a soul out of place,
watch me throw it,
can't feel beyond words
and you know it.

I'll take the time,
whatever I need,
I'll be as one,
I'll be damn free.

The flowers are watered,
the garden still grows,
your train of thought,
is what nobody knows.

I've felt the touch,
I've been there before,
it's a heart of gold
I want in a soul.

My Angel

My dear Crystal Ann,
I know you are there,
you have lifted my soul,
you always made me care.

That smile,
your innocent cry,
I felt God through your heart,
and know He is always nearby.

You are so much a blessing,
there has never been a doubt,
my heart is yours, sweet Crystal,
with yours I could never do without!

My Father

He leads us to follow the Lord
and says it shall be done.
Shinin' so bright
and lovin' all that have come.

They all have such a need,
and we feel it within,
smile, love, and reach
is where God's love begins.

So if He leads,
just follow your shine,
when you reach…
The heart of Jesus is mine.

Gift

A true gift has been given,
a real blessing has been reached,
do you even have any doubt,
in this time of your deepest need?

It's the faith in the hope we have,
in the miracles that always come,
a gift of life has been given,
do you see it,
or am I the only one?

Time

As time we see,
is time we grow,
take those chances,
don't be afraid to know.

Do you feel what I see,
are you moved ever so hard,
isn't that difficult to have,
what the others sometimes do not?

When you give,
most the time you get.
When you care,
most the time it's there.

If you're open to change
I know, as time we see,
is time we grow.

Change

Here it comes,
did you see it,
were you not watching,
when changes take place?
They don't ask if it's okay,
they want that look on your face.

Steer left, steer right,
maybe make it through the night,
plan a day,
hide away.

A change is coming,
it's time to pay.
So when it comes real fast,
look ahead and know,
it's not how well you take it,
but what you learn to finally let go.

Revelation

It truly is a revelation,
who we are in Christ,
given up the flesh and find a way
to let go of our vice.

Seems like no matter how hard we try,
we are just living to die,
and just finding the one who can answer
all those questions of why.

I pray, and pray, and pray,
and it is "I" that will never find the way,
to truly have that revolution in Christ,
I must die to the flesh each day.

My Dad

Where are those words when you just don't know,
a heart close to mine soon will be letting go.
Never to question why,
knowing my Lord will be close by.

So as words through our heart and I feel his pain inside,
my soul, guiding his path to the one that knows.
Never be at a loss for words
when it's your heart our God shows.

Humble

Humble are those that serve the Lord,
never running after riches,
never seeking that reward.
It's only that of love,
warms my heart to tears,
God gives me that humble path,
and will carry me through my years.

It's a promise our Lord gives to all,
when you seek and stay humble,
it's through our God Almighty
who would never let you stumble or fall.

I'm Not Far From Home

As I ease my thoughts through the day,
a smile is reached in every way.

I think about people who have lost their hope,
and always wonder why.
Really makes me ask why they never give life a try.

Sunsets, the sea, the moon, and sun,
these are all free to everyone.
Some can't see past their headlights,
even on the run,
slow down and look,
as your eyes enter in the sun.

So when I ease my thoughts,
I think of you,
and all that you share,
and feel all that you do.

Through me I will spread your word,
to those who want to know.
The few of us who listen,
someday will have a place to go.

Just Go

Go, man, go,
the vision is yours,
don't go slow--
We all have a purpose
I do know.

Go to bed late,
rise so early,
just finished the day
and fill what void?
A better way.

Sharpen your tools,
and keep them clean,
the tools of life
are often unseen.

When you run your thoughts,
they're always of go,
find some time,
find some slow.

If I had a day
that was mine to keep
I guess I've done it all,
now it's time to sleep.

Spilt Milk

I did what I said I wouldn't do,
I cried my guts out,
my guts out for you.

There's no rhyme
in the reason for this pain,
but the strength I hold within,
will be my angel once again.

Enjoy what you see
and always be free.
Don't cry over milk,
don't cry over me.

Far Away

When my mind drifts to a place far away,
It's of love, and peace, and you.
When I want to hold so close what we have,
to cry is all I can do.

I guess just wait 'til the angels of God start to sing.
Hope, desires, and life,
in your ears is all that will ring.

It's a feeling I want,
can't get there too soon,
for a real angel of love I would pray for the moon.

So let me drift to a place far away,
and dream I see your face,
past the stars someday.

Just Your Life

It's just your life,
can you see what's real?
Do you carry good,
in your heart how I feel?

Have you bared to your soul,
to all you can be,
have you lifted a heart,
to all it can reach?

The time grows long
for those with hate,
it's sad to think,
they're the ones our God won't take.

It's just your life
have you been given this real?
Trust in the Lord
it's Heaven I feel.

Hear to See

Ears to hear,
and eyes to see,
that's what our Lord wants
in you and truly wants in me.

He gives us what we should feel,
and how to lead your life,
sharing the Holy Spirit,
keeping the darkness from your sight.

Salvation is in our reach,
do you hear Jesus in your soul?
Eyes to see, and a heart that knows
it's the love of my Lord I feel,
it's my faith in Him that grows.

Melissa

I hear you're a star,
you have done good,
you're gonna go far.

Spread the word,
God is part,
sing your love,
show your heart.

You could sing a song,
about a place we know,
it's a place I dream,
the place I want to go.

It's a heaven above so far,
my eyes are clear,
I can surely see far.

Join my vision,
of this spiritual submission,
my voice, my heart,
in God I listen.

Precious Souls

Precious are the souls that love
and live pure in their heart,
all they know is give.

Tested every day,
as they work and pray,
never knowing a doubt,
that this is only God's way.

It's as simple as a smile,
that some don't see,
like holding the door,
as they walk out after me.

So warm, that precious soul,
the one that Jesus gives
as he calls on us to serve,
true souls are the ones that live!

Your Light

Does the Holy Spirit flow
through your veins,
are the decisions in your life,
the ones that will remain?

The choice to shine your light,
and give it all to those that can see.
If you carry the Holy Spirit,
your decisions will set you free.

So if you were to take that path of regret,
look back on the quick choice you made.
When the Holy Spirit is in you,
good decisions equal choice,
your light that shines only remains.

True Face

It's a time, it's a place,
just an age, not a face.
I've turned to you,
I've turned to be,
I've made the grade,
I'm hittin' fifty.

What I have seen,
and how I have lived,
not an age, not a face,
but measured in time,
how we give.

Is that it,
that's all there is to know,
in this space of time,
where we were taught to learn and grow?

Half a century down,
many decades left to go,
tomorrow should bring a why,
tomorrow will bring a know.
It's a time, it's a place,
not my age, just my face.

Lean

As I lean on my friends and God,
my faith is always reached,
it's a simple hope He will meet our needs.

When you're down, He's there,
He never lets you look away,
He trusts you know your heart,
and can feel what God has to say.

To forgive our sins is just the start,
Lean on God and faith's real hope,
good friends,
real love, starts only in the heart.

Share

Do you share what moves your heart,
always givin' your all, doin' your part?

It seems so simple to say,
"Hello, how are you today?"
only to hear, "Nuthin',"
and watch them walk away.

God sees the truth we feel!
He knows our heart,
He knows what's real.
Share what moves you
so your All is what you feel.

Choose

Are you the one that chooses to live,
are you the one that chooses to give?
When God puts your heart up for view,
will yours forever live and be a part of you?

I see right there, in front of me,
clear vision, and the rainbow,
there is no better place to be.

Choose to live,
choose to be,
when your heart's up for view
only God will see.

Jodi

There are many memories,
that lead us to love,
most the ones I feel,
are from my God, up above.

When you were young
and so full of why,
I gave you that chance,
to grow up and try.

You cannot fail in this game of life,
one Spirit, one hope,
real heart could never die.

Angel Hands

Words could never express,
of the vision that was sent...
The hand you give is the one you share...
A tear from an old woman,
reaching for her Lord,
to have Him show up to be there.

God's love in us at such a time
and such a place,
and the needed smile on my face
gave her the hope to know God's beside her.

My hand of love was from the Holy Spirit that day,
and an angel that night came to take her away.

My Friend

As we see our friends,
sometimes they come,
sometimes they go.

When their smile seems so real,
and they always have a laugh,
but it's their pain we cannot feel.

If you were to say
it's been nice to know you
these days we've had,
sharing the good,
forgetting the bad,
it would be God's journey for their life,
it will be their given plan.

So as we see our friends each day
as they come, and always seem to go,
be that friend that cares,
always let them know!

Just Pure

May your love be pure,
may your love be right,
this choice you have made to each other
is just the start to your life.

It's the give you share from your soul,
and never hold back the heart,
be pure with your love I say,
and enjoy this new start of your life.

Peace of Love

Piece of love is a piece of faith.
Share with me, Sweet Lord, a better day.

When these tears I cried are dried,
and I see Your face,
and You reaching for my hand
and saying I have a place.

It's a piece of Your love I feel in me.
Tears no more, my faith in You is there,
It's a piece of Your love,
It is that piece that You share.

Never Alone

My fears were answered,
by the strength of God.
My safe travels were in His plans,
He shared the path I was on.

It wasn't just the prayer,
to start my journey home,
it was the feeling through my heart
to know I was never to be alone.

So grab the Strength of God,
He will answer the path you are on.
Fears will be forgotten,
the Strength of God shall live on.

Soul Be True

Warm is hope,
hope is better,
a soul of troubled times
never gets to see God's letter.
It's been addressed to you all along,
the soul He wants to be true,
fills your heart,
a soul to be within you.

Hope is warm,
Lord willing
your soul is as true.

Humble Am I

How humble I,
I don't really know,
I feel your pain
and somehow so.

Your reach was real,
you have struggled much,
walk long harder
to stay in touch.

The different recipes and remedies
a many, you have the key,
you have always been ready.

You expressed your concerns,
and how it's all changed.
Follow these hopes,
and your dream still remains.

Who am I,
I don't know your pains.
I just think it's something,
the strength of all your gains.

We go through life
they say by day,
but what some endure
we all can't say.

So please smile and cry,
when it best fits you.
How humble am I,
I'll look to you.

Make Amends

Distance of friends who could know,
who would break and finally say,
what was in the back
of your mind that day
I say what do you know you know
what you don't.

Shake a hand, make amends,
try and see within your friends,
what they offer, what they're worth,
do they mean that much,
have they been friends since birth?

I guess look past,
it won't mean much.
I'll just be a friend
they say as such.

Have a beer,
share of hoot,
the music was loud,
then we got the boot.

Hey, look at you,
you're still my friend,
let's party awhile,
let's make amends.

Real

Not always easy,
to share what you feel,
starting to get closer,
starting to get real.

The fear of knowing
it might not work,
the hidden reality,
I just got took.

Don't share your lies,
put away that look,
it's my heart you see,
that should not be understood.

Time that grows
into time we see,
either I'm there for you,
or you're there for me.

Not always easy
to do what we feel,
'cause it's all about trust,
it's all about the real.

Gathering

I'm just gathering my love for another day,
my give is so powerful there is only one way.
It's through my heart I can feel,
my Lord's wishes are there,
He's calling on me, He is calling on you.

So just gather your love and have enough to give,
it just pours out of your soul,
and forever we shall live.
It's a gathering of friends, and family,
and the ones I know will be there.

The sun is shining,
Jesus is smiling,
it's a gathering of love,
it's a gathering of share.